MATT HAGEE

SPIRITUAL WARFARE

*Unlock the Supernatural
and Access the Promises of God*

Assembled and Produced for Hagee Ministries by
Breakfast for Seven
breakfastforseven.com

Printed in the United States of America.

TABLE OF CONTENTS

INTRODUCTION
The victory is yours!

Since the fall of man, there has been a war across the face of the earth that has never ceased, taking place in Heavenly places and impacting the lives of men and women. It is a battle in the unseen realm between the forces of good and those of evil. It is the age-old fight for the hearts and souls of men.

The topic of spiritual warfare is so vast that you can find it throughout Scripture. In the book of Job, we read a behind-the-scenes account of how the enemy was given permission to test Job's heart. At the end of Daniel's 21-day fast on the banks of the Tigris River, we learn how an angel contended with the "prince of the Persian kingdom" to get the message through (Daniel 10). And in the Gospels, Jesus repeatedly delivered many from evil spirits.

The battle was and remains spiritual. As it was in Jesus' day, so it is in ours, and spiritual warfare is still real. In Ephesians 6:10–13, Paul exhorts the church to be strong in the Lord and in the power of His might. He admonishes believers to put on the whole armor of God for the purpose of standing against the enemy and overcoming the power of darkness.

It is important to accept the fact that there is both the visible and the invisible. To our eyes, though God remains unseen, He is still real, and we still follow Him, love Him, and devote our lives to Him. John 4:24 reminds us that God is Spirit. There is the physical that we see and the spiritual that we do not see.

Spiritual warfare began when a third of the angels rebelled and were cast out of Heaven. It was a massive battle.

"And there was war in heaven, Michael and his angels waging war with the dragon. The dragon and his angels waged war, and they did not prevail, and there was no longer a place found for them in heaven. And the great dragon was thrown down, the serpent of old who is called the devil and Satan, who deceives the whole world; he was thrown down to the earth, and his angels were thrown down with him" (Revelation 12:7–9, NASB).

The accuser was cast out of Heaven and declared war on God's creation, those made in His image. And the battle will continue as long as the earth remains.

If you have not yet begun to fight, my hope and prayer is that this book will equip you with the tools you need to start fighting, to start praying in faith believing, and to start using praise to give God the glory for which He is worthy. I pray that you rise up in faith, silence all your enemies, and only move from one victory to the next.

It is time to start walking by faith and not by sight. It is time to become the warrior of faith that you are called to be. It is time to obtain the inheritance and good plans that the Lord has for you. And if you have been engaged in spiritual warfare and are familiar with the unseen battle that the enemy wages, this book will encourage you and spur you on to remain strong.

No matter what may come in life, you must never stop fighting. You must never stop waging war in the Heavenlies. You must never stop binding and loosing and advancing the Kingdom of God. Don't stop fighting for your unsaved loved ones, your marriage, or the dreams of your heart. Don't stop until the mountain moves, the giant falls, the fire is quenched, the sea is parted, and the victory is yours. In Christ, you are more than a conqueror.

Pastor Matt Hagee

MATT HAGEE | V

Section 1:
BECAUSE I SAID SO

RULES OF ENGAGEMENT

◇

You are from God, little children, and have overcome them;
because greater is He who is in you than he who is in the world.

1 JOHN 4:4, NASB

Spiritual warfare is a real conflict we are all engaged in. The warfare is real. It began before Genesis, it was there in the garden of Eden, and it persists upon the earth today. Spiritual warfare is not about you. It's about who gets the glory and who gets the praise. Will God be honored in your life? You can use spiritual warfare to silence the enemy's lies and accusations from taking root in your heart.

As a blood-bought believer, you have been authorized with the power of praise and prayer to conquer any spiritual adversaries that oppose you. With praise, you can silence the enemy. With prayer, you have the keys to bind and loose spiritual realities and to unlock the power of God's promise in your life.

You are not powerless on the earth. You have been bestowed with strength from on high to bind and loose and to place under supernatural arrest every power and principality that would attempt to hinder you, your home, or your finances from receiving the fullness of God's purposes and plans for you.

The difference between success or failure in spiritual warfare is based on your commitment to surrender to the promise and protection that come from following Christ. How far will you go in complete surrender to Jesus Christ? How abandoned will you be to lose your life for the sake of the Gospel and utter dependence on Him?

The difference between success or failure in spiritual warfare is based on your commitment to surrender to the promise and protection that come from following Christ.

What is warfare? Warfare is the engagement in conflict between opposing forces. By that definition, we are living in a world that is engaged in warfare on several fronts. Opposing forces are engaged in cultural warfare. We have seen protests, barricades, police in riot gear, and fights break out in the streets. Why? Opposing sides have drawn battle lines in cultural, social, and political warfare. Warfare is around us every day.

Regarding spiritual warfare, you are commanded to engage in the battle, and you can expect victory as the outcome. When it comes to the rules of engagement in spiritual warfare, you must understand the immense power you possess with your words. Proverbs 18:21 says,

"The tongue has the power of life and death" (NIV). Life and death are two drastic extremes.

Your Father in Heaven has empowered you with everything you need to defeat the enemy. You can overcome every obstacle and challenge, both spiritual and physical, because He has authorized you to be more than a conqueror through Christ Jesus. You can bind and loose. You can open doors or close doors. You can resist the enemy and cause him to flee. You can do all things through Christ who strengthens you.

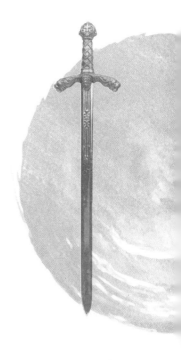

YOU'RE NOT THE ONLY ONE

◇

Having wiped out the handwriting of requirements that was against us, which was contrary to us. And He has taken it out of the way, having nailed it to the cross. Having disarmed principalities and powers, He made a public spectacle of them, triumphing over them in it.

COLOSSIANS 2:14–15, NKJV

When it comes to spiritual warfare, some choose to take the approach of denial. They say, "It's not real. It's just a scare tactic." But the Bible is clear that the supernatural world is just as real as the natural world. The Bible itself is a book of the supernatural, and the supernatural controls the natural.

Psalm 19:1 says, *"The heavens declare the glory of God; the skies proclaim the work of his hands"* (NIV). The natural lights we see in the sky — the sun, moon, and stars — are each controlled by the supernatural God who created them. He set them in place, He named each one, and they exist because it is His pleasure that they do so. All of creation must obey the commands of God.

The supernatural impacts what we see in our daily lives. When you see rebellion and lawlessness in the streets, when you see crowds of people out of control and enraged in their own minds — the reason they are is because they are being controlled by the supernatural forces of rebellion and lawlessness.

Every day you draw breath, you have a choice to make. You decide whose supernatural influence you are going to live under. Will you submit yourself daily to the influence of God Almighty, His Word that does not return void, and His Holy Spirit that provides peace, power, and comfort? Or will you give yourself to the influence of the world? Of self, the flesh, and the kingdom of darkness and evil?

The second you make your choice, you engage in the conflict between good and evil, light and darkness. Make no mistake, you do not get to opt out of the struggle, and there are no noncombatants in this fight. If you choose not to engage, you forfeit your opportunity to live a life of victory that Jesus Christ purchased for you with His shed blood at the Cross.

According to Colossians 2:15, on Calvary's hill, Jesus *"disarmed principalities and powers, He made a public spectacle of them, triumphing over them in it"* (NKJV). The enemy was decisively

> **If you choose not to engage, you forfeit your opportunity to live a life of victory that Jesus Christ purchased for you with his shed blood at the Cross.**

disarmed and defeated over 2,000 years ago. Now and today, you can live in victory over every lie and attack because of what Jesus has already accomplished.

Therefore, when it comes to spiritual warfare, the only way a blood-bought Christian can fail is if or when they refuse to take a stand against the enemy and remind him that, in the authority of Jesus' name and by the power of His Word, we are now covered in His shed blood and are more than conquerors through Christ Jesus (Romans 8:37).

THE NATURE OF THE STRUGGLE

◇

"The thief comes only to steal and kill and destroy; I came so that they would have life, and have it abundantly."

JOHN 10:10, NASB

When you recognize the nature of the struggle and what is going on behind the scenes, you begin to understand that this epic and cosmic battle started before you were born and will continue until God Almighty places the new Jerusalem on earth and Jesus sits on the throne (Revelation 21).

Until that day comes, you have a role to play. Psalm 150:6 says, *"Let everything that has breath praise the LORD. Praise the LORD!"* (NKJV). With the weapon of praise, you can significantly influence the life you live and the lives of the people around you. Your prayers and your worship can send the enemy fleeing as you give God highest praise.

This warfare is not a matter of who wins and who loses the final war, for that was determined at the Cross. But this warfare that we see on the earth decides who is going to get the glory in your everyday life. Are you, as a blood-bought believer, going to give God the glory He deserves with the sacrifice of praise? Or is the enemy going to put a stumbling block in front of you and cause you to be overwhelmed with doubt and fear and shrink back in timidity?

Do not let concern crush or drown your soul in fear. Even though the enemy comes as a thief to steal, you have a Great High Priest who makes intercession for you. He has overcome sin, death, and the grave, and He came that you would have life abundantly.

> **Even though the enemy comes as a thief to steal, you have a Great High Priest who makes intercession for you.**

Our God reigns forevermore. Our God is an awesome God who has already broken the power of the enemy. And now you have a great gift from your Heavenly Father. Second Timothy 1:7 says, *"For God has not given us a spirit of fear, but of power and of love and of a sound mind"* (NKJV). You can live your life and advance God's purposes on earth; for you have been endowed with these three great gifts.

Jesus said that you can live an abundant life. It's yours for the taking. You may have to wrestle it out of the hands of the enemy, but the good news is that you can. You have everything you need from on high to push back the darkness and walk in God's good plans and purposes for you.

You must never give up, and you must never settle. Give no ground to the deceiver, the serpent of old. The only way he gains ground in this type of warfare over your life is if you forfeit what Christ has won and placed in your hands. The enemy only steals, kills, and destroys.

But as for you, stand strong in the might of the Lord, resist the enemy, and begin to live in the shadow of God's powerful wings. As you remain close to Him, as the hymn says, *"The things of earth will grow strangely dim, in the light of His glory and grace."* [i]

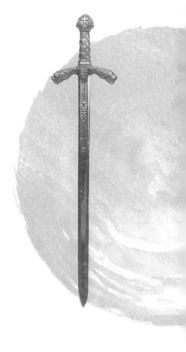

GOD KNOWS

---◇---

But he holds his priesthood permanently, because he continues forever. Consequently, he is able to save to the uttermost those who draw near to God through him, since he always lives to make intercession for them.

HEBREWS 7:24–25, ESV

God knows the fight you're in and why you're in it. The spiritual warfare you are in may be a surprise to you, but it didn't catch God by surprise. Remember, James 1:2–4 says, *"Count it all joy, my brothers, when you meet trials of various kinds, for you know that the testing of your faith produces steadfastness. And let steadfastness have its full effect, that you may be perfect and complete, lacking in nothing"* (ESV). God has never left you and will never leave you. He knows what you're going through, and He will always be right by your side.

Many of us want to be perfect and complete. But are we willing to be patient to get it? It's hard to struggle with a trial while we patiently wait for perfection. Sometimes we find ourselves in spiritual warfare, and we pretend we're the only ones who've ever suffered like this. We're in a battle, and we think God is just as shocked as we are.

But God is sovereign; not only did He already know about it, but He's all-powerful, meaning He allowed it! Consider the story of Job. Satan asked permission to test Job. God permitted it, but He also set limits on how far Satan could go. God said, *"Behold, he is in your power, only spare his life"* (Job 2:6, NASB). Job was indeed tested, but only within the limits God set.

The same thing happened to Peter. In Luke 22, Jesus says, *"Simon, Simon, behold, Satan demanded to have you, that he might sift you like wheat, but I have prayed for you that your faith may not fail. And when you have turned again, strengthen your brothers"* (v. 31–32, ESV). Satan went to God to obtain permission to test the disciples. But Jesus interceded in prayer.

Jesus knew Peter faced a major spiritual battle ahead. Satan didn't just sneak in and try to take down Peter without permission. He had to ask God to sift the disciples like wheat (v. 31). But Jesus told Peter that He was on his side when He said that He prayed for him.

You may be in the spiritual fight of your life, but the Son of the Living God is on your side. In the doctor's office, when you hear a diagnosis, He's on your side. In the boardroom, when the future of the business hangs in the balance, He's by your side. When you're searching for hope, He's by your side. He gives strength to the weary and increases the power of the weak. He is and always will be right by your side.

> **You may be in the spiritual fight of your life, but the Son of the Living God is on your side.**

Let Hebrews 7:25 become a continual encouragement to you: *"He is also able to save to the uttermost those who come to God through Him, since He always lives to make intercession for them"* (ESV). No matter how far gone you may feel, no matter what trial or difficulty you are in, right now and always, *"He is also able to save to the uttermost."*

WHO GETS THE GLORY?

◇

"The LORD will cause your enemies who rise against you to be defeated before your face; they shall come out against you one way and flee before you seven ways."

DEUTERONOMY 28:7, NKJV

The battle is about who gets the glory. When Satan unleashed Hell on Job, he was attempting to get Job to denounce the Lord. He wanted Job to forsake his faith and stop worshiping God, who created Heaven and earth.

And when the enemy did all he could to attack Job, Job said, *"The LORD gave, and the LORD has taken away; blessed be the name of the LORD"* (Job 1:21, ESV). Job refused to stop praising the Lord. He knew then what we must remember today — just because things may change on earth doesn't mean anything changes in Heaven.

The same God who blessed you in the past is still on the throne and worthy of your praise. The same God who conquered your enemies before is still mighty in battle. The same God you trusted the last time you were in need is still worthy of highest praise.

When you're in the midst of a struggle, you must remember the key to your breakthrough lies in direct correlation to how resilient you are in clinging to your faith. No matter what may happen in your life, never, ever stop giving the Lord praise. It's when you praise in the valley that you understand what Paul meant when he said to offer a sacrifice of praise (Hebrews 13:15).

A sacrifice costs you something; it isn't something easy to do. A sacrifice is an act of your will to lift your hands and say, "Lord, even though I don't see how any good can come from this, I'm going to praise Your name because you are still God."

A sacrifice of praise is a sweet aroma ascending to the halls of Heaven because it proclaims that you believe God is good; His lovingkindness is better than life; and His presence is the fullness of your joy. When you remember His overwhelming faithfulness, His enduring promises, and His true Word, you will strengthen your heart and rise in faith.

A sacrifice of praise is a sweet aroma ascending to the halls of Heaven...

So, when you feel alone, praise God and feel the reassurance of His presence. When you're brokenhearted, praise God and let Him bind up your wounds. When you're lost, praise God and follow Him as He makes your crooked ways straight. When you're in need, praise God for He's a Good Shepherd, a Faithful Provider, and a Strong Protector.

Forevermore, He is worthy; He is mighty to save; and He can heal, restore, and deliver. He is the glory and the lifter of your head, and there is none like Him. So today, lift your voice in praise. Declare His victory over every obstacle, mountain, and attack of the enemy. Thank Him for who He is and let the words of your mouth and the meditation of your heart be always pleasing in His sight.

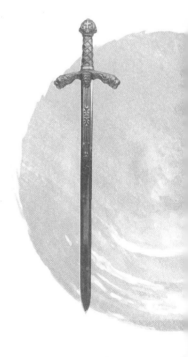

But those who wait on the LORD shall renew their strength;

they shall mount up with wings like eagles, they shall run and not be weary, they shall walk and not faint.

ISAIAH 40:31 (NKJV)

Section 2:

LIKE YOU HAVE NOTHING TO LOSE

TAKING GROUND

◇

"And I also say to you that you are Peter, and on this rock I will build My church, and the gates of Hades shall not prevail against it. And I will give you the keys of the kingdom of heaven, and whatever you bind on earth will be bound in heaven, and whatever you loose on earth will be loosed in heaven."

MATTHEW 16:18–19, NKJV

I want you to learn how to take ground in spiritual warfare. You and I were not redeemed from sin and given the authority of Jesus' name so that we would live on the defensive. We are not sitting ducks with targets on our backs, hoping that we have enough strength and willpower to keep the enemy at bay. Paul said, *"If the Spirit of Him who raised Jesus from the dead dwells in you, He who raised Christ Jesus from the dead will also give life to your mortal bodies through His Spirit who dwells in you"* (Romans 8:11, NASB). The same power that conquered death when Jesus rose from the grave is alive in you.

This not only means that when we find ourselves in a spiritual battle, we use praise to give God glory and silence the enemy, but according to the rules of engagement, we have been given authority by God Himself to win. We can now bind and loose, conquer and defeat, and advance in the conflict, so when the battle is over, we are indeed more than conquerors through Christ. We do not war according to the flesh, but our weapons can pull down strongholds, arguments, powers, and principalities. Commitment to warfare prayer is the weapon God has given you to gain ground in Heavenly places.

> **Commitment to warfare prayer is the weapon God has given you to gain ground in Heavenly places.**

Jesus said, *"From the days of John the Baptist until now the kingdom of heaven suffers violence, and the violent take it by force"* (Matthew 11:12, NKJV). When you engage in warfare prayer, you are engaging in a spiritually violent behavior in the authority of Jesus' name. It forces Hell and every power and principality to back up whenever you lift high the mighty name of Jesus.

The supernatural can control and influence the natural and what we do not see. We realize our battle is a supernatural one. It may manifest itself in a natural setting, but it is won or lost in the spiritual realm. We also must understand that the battle is a violent conflict, and the prize is the eternal destination of the souls of men and women.

The definition of violence is the use of physical force to injure, damage, or destroy. [ii] It is to disrupt with force or to hurt. This is exactly what the enemy intends to do to you. He wants to disrupt your emotional and spiritual well-being with force. He only knows how to steal, kill, and destroy your soul in such a way that he can keep you from any and every promise God has ever made to you through His Word, His Son, and His Holy Spirit.

But God has ordained you to drive the enemy out of your life, your marriage, your finances, your future, and your physical body in the authority of Jesus' name and by the power of His shed blood. You have the Biblical mandate from James 4:7, *"Submit yourselves therefore to God. Resist the devil, and he will flee from you"* (KJV). He has promised that He will *"soon crush Satan under your feet"* (Romans 16:20, NIV). Child of God, you are a part of the church triumphant, and victory is ours through Christ our Lord!

CURIOUS, CONVINCED, COMMITTED

———— ◇ ————

Trust in the LORD with all your heart, and lean not on your own understanding; in all your ways acknowledge Him, and He shall direct your paths.

PROVERBS 3:5–6, NKJV

When it comes to spiritual warfare and the topic of the supernatural, there are three groups of people. They are the curious, the convinced, and the committed. In the earthly ministry of Jesus, we see these three groups identify themselves time and time again.

Consider the day Jesus fed the 5,000. In the multitude of people who gathered to hear Him teach that day, the majority were curious. They wanted to see a man who could do miracles. Today, there are many who are curious when it comes to who Christ is. Some are curious to know why so many people are committed to Him. They want to know how He can make such a dramatic change in the lives of people who were once bound by sin. But you will never know the satisfaction and joy of the Lord until you are convinced that Jesus is not just another religious figure in whom some place their hope. Rather, He is the Son of the Living God.

There is only one name under Heaven by which God saves us: the mighty name of Jesus. His is the name that delivers the addict from the chains of addiction. His is the name that breaks the yoke of bondage. His is the name that makes the lame leap, the dumb speak, and the deaf hear again.

The name of Jesus comforts the afflicted. The name of Jesus conquers sickness and disease. The name of Jesus mends the brokenhearted. And the name of Jesus makes old things pass away and all things to become new again.

We must be convinced that His name is above every name. We must be convinced that His name makes a way where there seems to be no way. And that unto Him, every knee shall bow, and every tongue shall confess that Jesus Christ is Lord, to the glory of God the Father. Convincement then, must lead to commitment. Jesus is looking for the committed — those who are willing to say, "Lord, I am willing to give You everything I have so that You can take it and use it to meet a multitude of needs." It's time to say to God, "Whatever I have is Yours. Whatever You need, I'll give. Whatever you ask, I'll do. Wherever You send me, I'll go."

We must be convinced that His name makes a way where there seems to be no way.

The same Jesus who fed a crowd of 5,000 on a Galilean hillside with five loaves of bread and two fish is here and active in the world today. He's looking for the committed. He's looking for those who will love with all their heart, soul, mind, and strength. He's looking for those who will move beyond curiosity, past the point of even being convinced, and who have jumped with both feet into the waters of absolute commitment to Jesus Christ as Lord.

The believer who is fully devoted and 100% committed to God will fast and pray until God's power defeats every physical stronghold and sickness. They will work in the fields and share the Gospel with the lost. They will lift the banner of truth and take a stand in the evil day until every principality is conquered. To such as those, the Kingdom of Heaven awaits, for they will take God at His Word, believe Him wholeheartedly, and go and advance His purposes on the earth.

COMMISSIONED TO ADVANCE

⸻ ◇ ⸻

*"Truly I tell you, whatever you bind on earth
will be bound in heaven, and whatever you
loose on earth will be loosed in heaven."*

MATTHEW 18:18, NIV

A commission is a "warrant granting the power to perform various acts or duties." It is an "authorization or command to act in a prescribed manner or to perform prescribed acts." [iii] One gives a commission to officially charge the recipient with a responsibility. After Peter professed his commitment to Jesus by saying, *"Thou art the Christ, the Son of the living God"* (Matthew 16:16, KJV), Christ extended the commission to build His church to all those who would profess the same.

Every person who carries a commission wears the appropriate gear identifying who they are, what they are commissioned to do, and where they are authorized to do it. We see local police in the city, troopers across the state, and federal law enforcement across the country. As a committed child of God, He has commissioned you too in Heavenly places.

The Champion of Calvary, the Conqueror of death, Hell, and the grave endorses your authority as a believer in Christ. Jesus holds all authority in Heaven and earth, and to you He has said, *"I will give you the keys of the kingdom of heaven"* (Matthew 16:19, NKJV). Now, you possess the authority to bind and loose on earth. And what you do on earth will also be done in Heaven.

How will you use the keys God has given you? God has officially charged you, as a committed saint on the earth with the function of using His authority to gain ground in Heavenly places. The keys of the Kingdom of Heaven have the power to unlock healing, unlock deliverance, and establish the Kingdom because you can pull down strongholds that exalt themselves against the knowledge of God.

How will you use the keys God has given you?

There is so much available to you. And you are also not left alone in the dark without guidance regarding what your next step should be. Jeremiah 33:3 says, *"Call to Me, and I will answer you, and show you great and mighty things, which you do not know"* (NKJV). When you don't know what to do, call on His name. When you don't know where to go, call on His name. When you're out of strength, call on His name. He is a shelter in the storm and a friend who sticks closer than a brother.

You have the power of His name to receive all that you need. And who is this great King of kings and Lord of lords? He is the First and the Last; the Beginning and the End; the One who was and is and is to come. He is your Provider, Good Shepherd, Shelter, Healer, Great

Redeemer, and Friend. He can break every chain and set every captive free. He can make a way where there is no way. Why? Because He is supernatural. He is omnipotent. He is everlasting. He is God.

Stop waiting for God to move in your situation. He has already equipped you with what you need and commissioned you to go out and take ground. He has given permission, conferred authority, and issued marching orders. All that remains for you now is to "just start" and take the first step and move forward into God's purposes and plans for you to unlock Heaven and receive the victory, in Jesus' name!

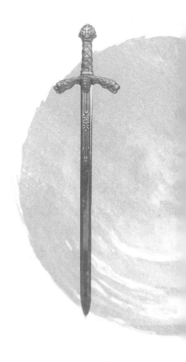

NOTHING TO LOSE

◇

Jesus replied: "'Love the Lord your God with all
your heart and with all your soul and with all your
mind.' This is the first and greatest commandment."

MATTHEW 22:37–38, NIV

You will embark on the greatest adventure of your life
when you finally let go, become fully sold out to Christ,
and live like you have nothing to lose. The challenge we
face when it comes to this type of commitment is that
we think we will lose more than we gain.

Consider what total commitment to Christ looks like.
It's not about you. It is about Him and Him alone. The
rich young ruler was convinced that Jesus was the One
to follow, but the price of commitment was greater than
he wanted to pay (Mark 10:17–27). He considered his
worldly riches of greater treasure than what following
Christ would offer him.

But listen to what Jesus said: *"If anyone desires to*
come after Me, let him deny himself, and take up his
cross, and follow Me. For whoever desires to save his life
will lose it, but whoever loses his life for My sake will find
it. For what profit is it to a man if he gains the whole

world, and loses his own soul?" (Matthew 16:24-26, NKJV). The key to finding true life then is in losing it for the sake of Christ.

Remember, the supernatural controls the natural. When you look at these verses with just your natural eyes, they become a difficult place to navigate because your focus is still on the world. But Jesus said that He came so you may have life and have it abundantly (John 10:10). He can open the floodgates of Heaven and pour out blessings upon you that you cannot contain (Malachi 3:10).

It's not about renouncing all your earthly possessions. Jesus wasn't saying, "Don't live your natural life. Don't try to do it all yourself and in your strength." He was saying, "Live your natural life in supernatural service to Me." Whatever you have in this life and all that you value — the only way to protect it is to give it to God. Find protection in obedience. Let Him use what you offer, bless it, and multiply it. Then trust Him to provide baskets full of all that you need.

Whatever you have in this life and all that you value — the only way to protect it is to give it to God.

Remember what Jesus said in John 15:5, *"I am the vine, you are the branches. He who abides in Me, and I in him, bears much fruit; for without Me you can do nothing"* (NKJV). Apart from Jesus, there is nothing of value and nothing that lasts. We must remain connected to Him. Do you want your family to be a household of faith? Give it to Jesus. Do you have a child or a spouse in the far country? Give them to Jesus.

You have the authority of His name, His Word, and His blood to drive the enemy out of your house. You can declare like Joshua, *"As for me and my house, we will serve the Lord"* (Joshua 24:15, ESV).

You have the keys to unlock the promise of His Word in the lives of your children. You can bind every power, principality, and generational curse in Jesus' name. You can declare the blessings of Abraham, Isaac, and Jacob over their lives. You can say, "My children are the inheritance of the Lord. They don't belong to this fallen world. They don't belong to the spirit of the age. They belong to God Almighty, and God will use them for His glory in their generation!" You have all the authority you need to evict the enemy from your house, take back what he has stolen, and consecrate your house to God.

FULLY SURRENDERED

◇

Draw near to God, and he will draw near to you. Cleanse your hands, you sinners, and purify your hearts, you double-minded.

JAMES 4:8, ESV

Gaining ground in the Kingdom of God is a matter of never giving up. Once you are convinced that Christ is the way the truth and the life, the only way to gain ground is to commit yourself to giving up all you have to Him.

Satan wants you to believe that you can't, but God has promised that if you lose your life for His sake, you will find it. So how do you not give up any ground? The first step is to not lay down and let the enemy walk all over you. You can't be passive in this supernatural fight for your life. Begin your day by kneeling and surrendering your life anew each morning to God.

The enemy wants the glory of your life. Not only does he want you to stop praising God, but he also wants to keep you from reaching out to God in prayer. He wants to silence you, distract you, and fill you with the cares of this life's riches so that you take your eyes off the true prize, which is Christ alone.

Satan doesn't hold the keys to death and Hades; Jesus does (Revelation 1:18). The enemy doesn't have the power to bind and loose; you do (Matthew 18:18). The enemy is the father of lies. He can whisper in your ear, "There's nothing you can do about it," but that is not true in the slightest. You must come to the place where you take the Bible at its word and believe the words that you read. When you believe, really believe and live like you do, everything changes.

Believe the promises in Scripture that tell you who you are in Christ. Read them, memorize them, and repeat them over and over. Say to yourself, "Yes. I believe the words of this book. And yes, I can do what Jesus has said I can do." In faith believing, you can go into Heavenly places in the power of Jesus' name, and you can be victorious. You can overcome, and you can live as more than a conqueror on the earth.

When you believe, really believe and live like you do, everything changes.

The riches of Christ are available to you. They are not far off. But as one who has been grafted in, they are your birthright. The only thing that separates you from what is yours is your belief that they are for you. Right now, you can have peace which surpasses understanding. You can have the joy of the Lord, which is your strength. You can sit at a table prepared for you, even in the presence of your enemies. You can live a victorious life in Christ and defeat the giants that rise against you in Jesus' name.

You must believe. You must let go of this world. You must lay hold of Christ and Christ alone. Now is the time to live fully committed to His truth, His way, and His life. Today is the day of salvation, and now is the time for redemption and restoration. Choose today to completely, finally, utterly surrender to His will.

In Jesus' name, you can. By the power of Christ, you can overcome every lie, every attack, and every power and principality that has stood against your life. You can enjoy the goodness of God in the land of the living. And you can possess His promises for you, right here and right now. Today, let God arise, and may His enemies scatter!

In my distress I called upon the L<small>ORD</small>*, and cried out to my God; He heard my voice from His temple, and my cry came before Him, even to His ears. Then the earth shook and trembled;*

the foundations of the hills also quaked and were shaken, because He was angry.

PSALM 18:6–7 (NKJV)

Section 3:

I'VE GOT YOUR BACK

THE GREATEST CHALLENGE

--- ◇ ---

*Finally, my brethren, be strong in the Lord and in the power
of His might. Put on the whole armor of God, that you may
be able to stand against the wiles of the devil. For we do not
wrestle against flesh and blood, but against principalities,
against powers, against the rulers of the darkness of this age,
against spiritual hosts of wickedness in the heavenly places.
Therefore take up the whole armor of God, that you may be
able to withstand in the evil day, and having done all, to stand.*

EPHESIANS 6:10–13, NKJV

There is a great challenge we face as Bible-believing
Christians. It is the greatest failure in the body of
Christ, and it is the primary reason why the enemy has
a foothold in our culture, our families, our schools, and
every other area of our society. The problem is not that
we don't know the principles of spiritual warfare, and it
is not because the powers of Hell are too strong for us
to conquer and overcome. The problem is: the body of
Christ is not unified.

Jesus, our Commander and Chief, didn't conquer sin,
death, Hell, and the grave at Calvary to start 101 denom-
inations that argue and debate about who is going to get

into the gated community of Heaven first. He died and rose victorious on the third day for more than that!

What did He pray? He prayed: *"For those who will believe in Me through their word; that they all may be one, as You, Father, are in Me, and I in You; that they also may be one in Us, that the world may believe that You sent Me. And the glory which You gave Me I have given them, that they may be one just as We are one: I in them, and You in Me; that they may be made perfect in one, and that the world may know that You have sent Me, and have loved them as You have loved Me"* (John 17:20–23, NKJV).

Jesus prayed that the church would be unified and made perfect as one. Why? So the world may know who God is and what Jesus has already accomplished. The devil cannot beat, knock down, or destroy a unified church. Rather, a unified church can triumph over sickness and disease, powers and principalities, and chains of bondage and addiction.

A unified church can put 10,000 to flight. When we are one, we are unstoppable. When we gather in His name and agree concerning anything, mountains of need move and rivers of restoration flow from Heaven's throne. When we gather in prayer like the disciples did in the upper room, the Holy Spirit's power can destroy strongholds as we lift the mighty name of Jesus.

> **The devil cannot beat, knock down, or destroy a unified church.**

A united church lifts His name above every name, shines the light of Jesus in a dark generation, and walks in the power and glory of God Almighty. We must work towards unity within the body of Christ; for when we are one, we can powerfully pierce the darkness and win many souls to the saving grace of Jesus, our Lord.

STRATEGIES OF THE ENEMY

◇

"Behold, I give you the authority to trample on serpents and scorpions, and over all the power of the enemy, and nothing shall by any means hurt you."

LUKE 10:19, NKJV

God has defeated the devil, but it doesn't mean the devil isn't working overtime to do all he can to steal what he can from your life and take you down with him. Often, we make the mistake of giving the devil too much credit and blame everything that is wrong in our lives on him, or we ignore him and remain oblivious to his schemes.

Yes, the devil wants to steal, kill, and destroy, but he's not everywhere all the time. Some trouble we experience in our lives comes from self-inflicted wounds. These are the things in our lives that could heal if we would change our behavior rather than blame that old serpent.

The other mistake we make is the exact opposite. It is being spiritually insensitive. We become spiritually numb and don't pay any attention to what the devil is doing at all. We either refuse to take a stand or ignore the opportunity to engage in the battle right in front of us.

You must not remain spiritually blind to the devil's handiwork. You must be aware that the devil doesn't just work against the church; he also works in the church. Every Sunday when the pastor declares the truth of God's Word, spiritual forces are at work, doing all they can to divide and conquer. These forces want to take the whole truth of God's Word and keep it from taking root in your life so they can conquer you.

You come to church and hear, "You can do all things through Christ," and immediately spiritual forces sneak in and sow division and doubt. You may hear principles for godly marriages or how to draw near to God, and spiritual attacks come and try to choke out these seeds of truth and hope.

Paul clearly encourages believers in Ephesians 6 to *"be strong in the Lord and in the strength of His might. Put on the full armor of God, so that you will be able to stand firm against the schemes of the devil"* (vv. 10–11, NASB). It's not a full-on attack; rather, it's a series of doubtful, divided thoughts intended to keep individuals isolated and vulnerable. These are the wiles, schemes, and tricks of the devil.

You come to church...and immediately spiritual forces sneak in and sow division and doubt.

We must *"take up the full armor of God"* (v. 13) so that we can stand and resist what comes against us. You must recognize your responsibility to put on the armor made available to you. God and His living Word provide every piece, but whether you wear it is your choice. It's not

God's responsibility to dress you. He provided the armor but, in faith for each day, you must dress yourself. This is how you trample on serpents and scorpions and overcome the power of the enemy.

FOUNDATION OF TRUTH

◇

*...Jesus said, "If you hold to my teaching, you
are really my disciples. Then you will know the
truth, and the truth will set you free."*

JOHN 8:31–32, NIV

Knowing the truth is how you gain freedom from what has
held you back. Paul admonished the church to stand fast
and to gird our waists with truth (Ephesians 6:14). We are
to wrap truth around us like a belt. Truth is the foundation
of the spiritual armor that every believer can wear. The
Greek word for truth is *Aletheia*. It means "verity, truth,
sincerity, or divine truth revealed to man." [iv] It is being
honest and straightforward.

The foundation of every Christian's life should be
the honesty and sincerity of their character. Their word
should be completely dependable. Living your life with
Aletheia means having the willingness to be who you
fully are in Christ.

Honesty is the foundation. The body of Christ will
never have the proper foundation for victory until we are
willing to be honest and sincere about our strengths and
weaknesses. It is when we can love one another and not

take advantage of others' weaknesses. When we encourage and build one another up based on mutual love and respect instead of out of a need to compete, we love with a sincere form of love.

When we do that, we can really love one another in truth. There's no point in pretending because we can't hide anything from God anyway. Why not be honest and real, and tell the truth to those with which we are in community?

When you're honest, you give God operating room where He can go to work on your situation. He can mend what's been mangled; He can cut what needs to be pruned; and He can reconstruct and heal the broken pieces in your life. If you continue to mask how you're really doing with empty spiritual words, the enemy still has a foothold in your life.

> **When you're honest, you give God operating room where He can go to work on your situation.**

Be honest with God about where you are in life. Being honest about what's going on in your life, with God, and with others, keeps the enemy from being able to sow division in your heart and emotions. Truth and honesty are like beacons that shine through the soul, illuminating corners of darkness and bringing all things to the light.

Truth brings freedom. Romans 1:16 says, *"I am not ashamed of the gospel of Christ, for it is the power of God to salvation for everyone who believes, for the Jew first and also for the Greek"* (NKJV). You have no righteousness outside of your relationship with Jesus Christ. But you can't accept this truth unless you're covered in the truth of your need for the love and mercy of God.

Search for truth in God's Word. You will find freedom from oppression and the bondage of the enemy when you reject his lies and accept the mercy of God toward you. And on that day, truth will usher you into a new level of freedom.

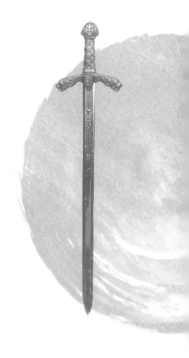

MOVING IN VICTORY

◇

Stand therefore, having girded your waist with truth, having put on the breastplate of righteousness, and having shod your feet with the preparation of the gospel of peace; above all, taking the shield of faith with which you will be able to quench all the fiery darts of the wicked one.

EPHESIANS 6:14–16, NKJV

You can live in a place of victory over the enemy. When you are clothed appropriately with the armor of God, you can withstand his fiery darts. The breastplate of righteousness protects the heart. This is important because Proverbs 4:23 says, *"Above all else, guard your heart, for everything you do flows from it"* (NIV). Out of the heart spring the issues of life. If your heart is spiritually sick, it can lead to a spiritually sick life as well.

When you put on the breastplate of righteousness, you protect your heart, your motives, and the reason you do what you do. When we store up God's Word in our hearts, we guard against sin (Psalm 119:11). We use God's Word as a light to our feet and a lamp to our path more easily when we are not bogged down by the burden of living in sin.

Gird your feet with the Gospel of peace. The message we carry is not our message. It's His message. It's the Gospel of peace. It's His Gospel that breaks the chains of sin. It's His Gospel that delivers and heals. It's His Gospel that conquers the enemy.

Above all, take up the shield of faith. Faith is the victory that overcomes the world. Faith is paramount to obtaining freedom in your life, for the righteous shall live by faith (Romans 1:17). Moreover, without faith it is impossible to please God (Hebrews 11:6). Faith is daring your soul to see further than your natural eye can see. Faith challenges your mind to believe what is impossible to understand in the natural. Faith is behaving like you believe what the Bible says, for all things are possible for the one who believes (Mark 9:23).

The helmet of salvation is a right mind. It is a mind kept in perfect peace because it focuses on God and trusts fully in Him (Isaiah 26:3–4). Paul said, *"I am not ashamed, for I know whom I have believed and am persuaded that He is able to keep what I have committed to Him until that Day"* (2 Timothy 1:12, NKJV). He committed his thoughts to the fact that no matter what happened, he was saved, forgiven, and sheltered in the loving arms of God.

Faith is daring your soul to see further than your natural eye can see.

You can do the same. You can commit your mind to think on *"whatever is true, whatever is honorable, whatever is just, whatever is pure, whatever is lovely, whatever is commendable, if there is any excellence, if there is anything worthy of praise"* (Philippians 4:8, ESV). As you do, you will renew your mind and recalibrate your heart to the things above. Your eyes will shift to Heaven, and the knowledge of what Jesus has already accomplished will bring freedom to your soul.

THE SWORD OF THE SPIRIT

Yet Michael the archangel, in contending with the devil, when he disputed about the body of Moses, dared not bring against him a reviling accusation, but said, "The Lord rebuke you!"

JUDE 1:9, NKJV

The Word of God is the Sword of the Spirit. You can weaponize your words in the supernatural realm by picking up your Bible every day and declaring what it says over you, your life, and the lives of those you love. The Word of God is living, and it is active. It does not return void. When the Word of God enters a situation, that situation must bend and conform to come into alignment with the Word.

When the enemy comes to attack, he uses doubt and desire to try to knock you off track and entice you to fall into temptation. He can't force you to do anything, but he can lie and deceive. Consider his tactics in Matthew 4, when Jesus faced temptation in the wilderness. After 40 days, Satan came and tempted Jesus with doubt and physical desire. Matthew 4:3, *"If you are the son of God* (doubt), *command that these stones become bread* (desire)" (NKJV).

Jesus combated Satan's devices by the Word of God. Three times He said, *"It is written."* When Jesus wielded the Sword of the Spirit, Satan could not stand. He drove Satan away from Him and overcame each temptation by quoting the Word of God.

How does the enemy tempt you? He wants you to doubt what God said and uses your natural desire to drive you to do your will and not God's will. You must learn to do what Jesus did. You don't have to square off and attack the enemy head-on in your own strength. The battle is in the Heavenlies, and the Word of God holds the final say.

If quoting the Word of God is what Jesus did, it is the best course of action you can take as well. And if you are going to be able to quote the Word, you must know the Word. You must get the Word in you before it can come out of you. You must wear it, read it, live it, and speak it daily!

The devil will never leave you alone because he feels sorry for you. He doesn't give up because you've gotten emotional. He will only flee when you declare the Word. And if you are in a situation where you feel an attack of the enemy and you can't recall any verses in the moment, picture Jesus on the Cross in your mind's eye and repeat His name over and over. It will calm you down and cause the enemy to flee. Then you can open your Bible, find a verse, and stand on the written Word.

> **If quoting the Word of God is what Jesus did, it is the best course of action you can take as well.**

Read His promises over and over and put on the armor of God daily. Take His living Word, focus on it, and cast down every thought that exalts itself against the knowledge of God. And remember, *"You are of God, little children, and have overcome them, because He who is in you is greater than he who is in the world"* (1 John 4:4, NKJV).

"The LORD will cause your enemies

who rise against you to be defeated before your face;

they shall come out against you one way and flee before you seven ways."

DEUTERONOMY 28:7 (NKJV)

Section 4:

TAKE A CLOSER LOOK

CELESTIAL EVANGELISTS

$\diamond$

When I consider Your heavens, the work of Your fingers, the
moon and the stars, which You have ordained, what is man that
You are mindful of him, and the son of man that You visit him?

PSALM 8:3–4, NKJV

On December 25th, 2021, a next-generation telescope
called the James Webb Space Telescope launched on an
Ariane 5 rocket from Kourou, French Guiana. A collab-
oration between 14 countries — NASA, the European
Space Agency, and the Canadian Space Agency — came
together to create a brand-new telescope that has since
sent back never-before-seen images from deep space. v

Astronomers have now looked so far into outer space,
they are saying they can see lights that were shining
when the earth and the sun began. They've never been
able to see them before. This telescope took 30 years and
$10 billion to build. One scientist on the project reported
that the galaxies they're viewing now have always been
in existence — they just weren't able to see them because
they didn't have a telescope powerful enough.

The Webb Telescope has sent back utterly amazing
images, and this capability is an incredible technological

breakthrough. But the telescope only confirms what the Word of God has already said. They could have saved a lot of time and money by reading Psalm 19:1, *"The heavens declare the glory of God; the skies proclaim the work of his hands"* (NIV). Since creation, the sun, moon, and stars have been set in place as celestial evangelists, burning, flickering, and shining on a 24-hour-a-day basis, telling us our God is an awesome God.

There is always more to learn and see. But what happens in the unseen world that God has created? All around us, there is spiritual warfare taking place. There are angels of the Living God, and there are demonic forces of Hell. And every day, they're clashing with each other. It's an unseen spiritual reality, but it impacts our lives.

The reality of a spiritual world at work all around us is real, whether we see it or not. Just like the images from the Webb Telescope that show us new stars we have never seen before, in the same way, there are spiritual realities at work on earth even though we do not see them. But the Word of God tells us how to live, in light of the reality of the seen and the unseen. It is a powerful tool that shows us the seen and unseen world that we're living in and helps us understand that, despite how things may seem, the unseen hand of God is ever working on our behalf.

> **The reality of a spiritual world at work all around us is real, whether we see it or not.**

God's plan is to bless you, prosper you, and keep you in all your ways. He is the God who calls those things that are not as though they were. You may not be able to see it, and you may not be able to grasp it, but the eyes of the Lord are everywhere and in every place. And as you tune your heart to the Word of God and draw near to Him in faith believing, you will discover God's plan for you to rise in victory in both the seen and unseen in every area of your life.

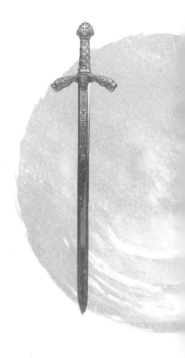

UNSEEN REALITIES

◇

*For by him all things were created, in heaven and on earth,
visible and invisible, whether thrones or dominions or rulers or
authorities — all things were created through him and for him.*

COLOSSIANS 1:16, ESV

Our lives are filled with unseen realities, and they impact
our daily lives. There are supernatural forces and principalities which exist and influence situations and life here on
earth. Paul tells us that there are certain things we will see
with our natural eye, but there are also things in existence
we cannot see because God created them invisible. These
things are real, but you just can't see them.

It took a team of thousands of scientists, engineers,
astronomers, and technicians 30 years and billions of
dollars to confirm what Romans 1:20 has already told us.
They're looking through a modern marvel of a telescope,
and they're seeing galaxies shining and saying this light
comes from when the world began. Well, here's what
Romans 1:20 says: *"For since the creation of the world His
invisible attributes are clearly seen"* (NKJV).

One very astute and acclaimed astronomer from the
University of Washington said that in his decades of study,

he had never seen such spectacular lights. "As a matter of fact," he said, "I am ecstatic at the scientific prospects of this new telescope. I should say gobsmacked!" [vi] I've never heard such a fancy way to say "speechless."

What caused this Ph.D. in astronomy to be gobsmacked? He got just one glimpse of the awesome glory of God on display. When he saw what wonderful things God could do, he was simply awed. Creation itself proved once again that the sun, moon, and stars proclaim the glory of God — ever burning, flickering, and shining 24 hours a day.

Day and night, all that God has made proclaims that our God is an awesome God. Psalm 19:1 says, *"The heavens declare the glory of God; the skies proclaim the work of his hands"* (NIV). God Almighty is enthroned in the highest Heavens. He rules as King above kings and Lord above lords. He is omnipotent and omniscient beyond our comprehension. Psalm 147:4 says, *"He counts the number of the stars; He calls them all by name"* (NKJV).

Day and night, all that God has made proclaims that our God is an awesome God.

Stars we can't even see, God has named and numbered. Galaxies we can't fathom, He formed and set in place. He created planetary nebulae, constellations, stars, moons, and planets, and set each one in space. He is so much greater than we can ever know in this life. He is the God who holds the mountains in a scale and the seas in the palm of His hands. Our God speaks to dust, and it lives. Our God calls those things that are not as though they were. In Isaiah 45:5–7, God says: *"I am the LORD, and there is no other, besides me there is no*

God; I equip you, though you do not know me, that people may know, from the rising of the sun and from the west, that there is none besides me; I am the LORD, and there is no other. I form light and create darkness; I make well-being and create calamity; I am the LORD, who does all these things" (ESV). Though we are not able to see it, the eyes of the Lord are everywhere and in every place.

Paul said, *"Do not look at the things which are seen, but at the things which are not seen. For the things which are seen are temporary, but the things which are not seen are eternal"* (2 Corinthians 4:18, NKJV). Learn to live through your eyes of faith, for the unseen is greater than the seen.

A BIBLICAL WORLDVIEW

---- ◇ ----

"In him we live and move and have our being"; as even some of your own poets have said, "For we are indeed his offspring."

ACTS 17:28, ESV

The Christian life is a matter of living with a Biblical worldview versus a secular worldview. And when you have a Biblical worldview, that means that the Bible tells you everything that you need to know about the life that you're living. If it's in the Book, you believe it, and then you behave like you believe because what you believe affects how you see the world and how you live your life.

There are a lot of people walking around who say, "I believe the Bible," but they don't behave like they believe. It takes faith to believe the words of the Book, and it takes faith to organize your life around what you read. But faith is not ethereal. Hebrews tells us that *"Faith is the substance of things hoped for, the evidence of things not seen"* (Hebrews 11:1, NKJV).

Your faith is built whenever you begin to see with your natural eyes how God's promises happen in your life. Your faith in God's Word goes out in front of you. And then, when you see His Word come alive, you begin to recognize that there is something in this Book that has real power. This is why Paul could say, *"I am not ashamed, for I know whom I have believed, and I am convinced that he is able to guard until that day what has been entrusted to me"* (2 Timothy 1:12, ESV).

Paul wasn't saying, "I guess, and I wonder." He had experienced enough of the reality of God in his life that he was 100% certain. He was persuaded beyond any doubt that God was able to keep what Paul had committed to Him. Do you know God like that?

If you have a secular worldview, it is easy to look at the world we're living in, hear about crisis after crisis, and have your senses immediately go into overdrive as you hear about rising inflation and challenges in the economy. But if you have a Biblical worldview, you believe that *"God shall supply all your need according to His riches in glory by Christ Jesus"* (Philippians 4:19, NKJV). You can look at Psalm 37:25 and take hope, for it says, *"I have not seen the righteous forsaken or his descendants begging for bread"* (NASB).

> **We may go through the worst of times, but because our God is so sufficient, we will have the best of things.**

We may go through the worst of times, but because our God is so sufficient, we will have the best of things because that's what His Word promises. He will never leave you nor forsake you. He will never abandon you nor leave you alone. He is your Good Shepherd, the Author and Perfector of your faith, and your Heavenly Father.

Though the trials of life may buffet your heart and the enemy may launch a siege against your soul, you can echo the psalmist who said, *"I will lift up my eyes to the hills — from whence comes my help? My help comes from the Lord, who made heaven and earth. He will not allow your foot to be moved; He who keeps you will not slumber. Behold, He who keeps Israel shall neither slumber nor sleep"* (Psalm 121:1–4, NKJV). Let your heart be strengthened today, for the King of all upholds you with His righteous right hand.

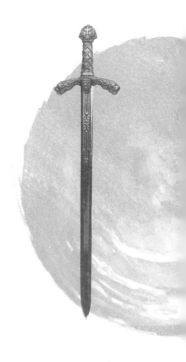

WHAT ARE YOU VIEWING?

―――――――― ◇ ――――――――

He loves righteousness and justice; the earth is full of the good-
ness of the LORD. By the word of the LORD the heavens were
made, and all the host of them by the breath of His mouth.

PSALM 33:5-6, NKJV

Your perspective on life is a powerful force that shapes
your decisions. The question you must continually ask
yourself is, "What am I viewing? What's shaping my
perspective?" Are you only paying attention to the visible
things that you can see or feel? Or are you looking at the
world and your life through the lens of God's Word?

When you recognize that His Word is alive, His
Word is powerful, and His Word will not return void,
your perspective changes. You find the strength to keep
going when you couldn't before. You find the hope to get
back up again when life has knocked you off your horse.
When you read it, God's Word is health to your navel and
marrow to your bones.

The Word of God is more powerful than any weapon
man ever conceived. His Word, when you speak it, is
sharper than any two-edged sword. His Word spoke the
world and the planets into existence. His Word, from

beginning to end, is everlasting. And His Word will give you the victory, in Jesus' name!

Just look at His Word and you'll find a God who has love that comes without limit. Look at His Word and you'll find a God whose mercy is renewed every morning. Look at His Word and you'll discover that where sin did abound, grace abounded even more. Look at His Word and you'll find a name that is above every name.

The mighty and matchless name of Jesus Christ, our God, is great beyond comprehension. He is the Lord of Glory, the Bright and Morning Star, and our Father in Heaven. We cannot contain Him in a temple or a sanctuary. We cannot capture Him in paintings or artwork. We cannot carve Him into a pile of stone.

We cannot lock Him up, argue Him out, debate Him, or confine Him on a campus or in a classroom. Our God is great and greatly to be praised! He determines the number of the stars and calls them each by name (Psalm 147:4). He is worthy of all praise — so much so that even the rocks of the earth would cry out in praise if man were silent (Luke 19:40).

To this day, the rocks still testify. You don't think so? Go to the Grand Canyon. It's talking to you. It's testifying, "God did this." He took just one of His fingers and drug it in the ground and look what He made. Paul said, *"Since the creation of the world His invisible attributes, that is, His eternal power and divine nature, have been clearly perceived, being*

> **To this day, the rocks still testify. You don't think so? Go to the Grand Canyon.**

understood by what has been made, so that they are with-out excuse" (Romans 1:20, NASB). Creation, as we know it, is a megaphone that continually testifies of God's power to the entire world.

THE FAITHFULNESS OF GOD

◇

The Lord appeared to us in the past, saying: "I have loved you with an everlasting love; I have drawn you with unfailing kindness."

JEREMIAH 31:3, NIV

God is so faithful. He's so good that we're surrounded by it to the point where we take it for granted. Imagine if God was inconsistent. For example, people in Texas are concerned about the power grid and that we could run out of power. Well, imagine if God got up tomorrow and decided that the sun was just going to take a day off.

Or if He said, "I wonder how long they'd last without oxygen." He's so consistent that we live our lives and don't even engage the idea that God is helping us. If you want to know what God does, read Job 38. In that discourse, God begins to speak with Job because Job questioned God and wanted to know why he went through his trials.

But God sets the stage, and Job very quickly sees his place. *"Then the Lord answered Job out of the whirlwind, and said: 'Who is this who darkens counsel by words without knowledge? Now prepare yourself like a man; I will question you, and you shall answer Me'"* (Job 38:1–3, NKJV). Then, from chapters 38 to 41, the Lord of all the earth questioned Job.

"Where were you when I laid the foundations of the earth?" (38:4). *"Where is the way to the dwelling of light?"* (38:19). *"Have you given the horse strength?"* (39:19). *"Can you draw out Leviathan with a hook…?"* (41:1). The King of Glory asked Job, *"Shall the one who contends with the Almighty correct Him?"* (40:2, NKJV). And Job was speechless.

At the end, all Job could say was, *"I know that You can do everything, and that no purpose of Yours can be withheld from You. You asked, 'Who is this who hides counsel without knowledge?' Therefore I have uttered what I did not understand, things too wonderful for me, which I did not know"* (Job 42:1–3, NKJV).

I've seen Him do too many incredible things for me not to take a moment and give Him glory. I've seen Him wash away too many sins for me not to be thankful for His forgiveness and grace. I've seen Him change too many lives for me not to give Him glory for the way He's been good to us. He has poured out His mercy and His grace without measure.

> **I've seen Him do too many incredible things for me not to take a moment and give Him glory.**

His favor has opened doors that no one could open. It's made a way where there could be no way! He's moved too many mountains, defeated too many enemies, and poured out more than we can contain! He's so faithful.

He's never forsaken us, and He's always forgiven us, time and again. He loves us with an everlasting love. When the sun comes up in the morning, I've got to give Him glory. And when the moon glows at night, I've got to give Him praise. And when the wind blows, I've got to say, "Thank You, Lord." I will celebrate His faithfulness and His goodness because the earth is the Lord's and the fullness thereof!

GIVING GOD GLORY

◇

Therefore, whether you eat or drink, or
whatever you do, do all things for the glory of God.

1 CORINTHIANS 10:31, NASB

Everyone on earth has wondered at one time or another
what their purpose is. People look in all manner of places
to find their purpose, but the reality is that it is only
found in God. Isaiah 43:7 says, *"Everyone who is called by*
My name, whom I have created for My glory; I have formed
him, yes, I have made him" (NKJV). That means that if
you were created by God, you were created for His glory.
Anyone living for any other reason than the glory of God
doesn't know why they exist.

In the beginning of time, before the earth was
formed, God created angels. And the purpose of the
angels was to give God glory. But the Bible tells us that
one third of those angels refused to give God glory.
They were deceived by another angel named Lucifer,
who wanted to take some glory for himself. And
when they didn't give God glory, God cast them out
of Heaven and, as fallen angels, they became demons
(Ezekiel 28:12–19; Revelation 12).

Based on that scriptural reality, to give God glory is to act as angels act. To not give God glory is to behave demonically. Your life on earth is about giving God glory. The Bible tells us, *"Whether you eat or drink, or whatever you do, do all to the glory of God"* (1 Corinthians 10:31, ESV). The key to this verse is to understand that "do all" means "do all."

Now oftentimes, people want to say, "Well, I don't understand how my life gives God glory." But it doesn't matter exactly what you do. This verse uses food and drink as an example because eating and drinking are the basic functions of every human being. Every one of us eats, and every one of us drinks. It's not so much about your diet as it has to do with everything you do. Whatever you do in this life, put God in front of it. Whatever business you're in, put God in front of it. When you get up in the morning at your home, put God in front of your marriage and your family. Put God in front of your decisions. Give God glory by putting Him first in all you do!

Whatever you do in this life, put God in front of it.

Everything you eat, everything you drink, everything you touch, everywhere you go, acknowledge God's involvement in it. God gave you every talent you have. God gave you every treasure you possess. He's the One who gives the power to get wealth, and He's the One who blessed you with it because all of the gold and all of the silver are His. He structured every breath that you breathe and the system in the atmosphere that enables you to inhale and exhale, which is why the Bible says, *"Let everything that has breath praise the LORD"* (Psalm 150:6, NIV).

When you acknowledge God in all you do, put Him first, and do all as unto Him, you live a life that gives God glory. In John 15:5, Jesus said, *"I am the vine, you are the branches. He who abides in Me, and I in him, bears much fruit; for without Me you can do nothing"* (NKJV). If you want to position yourself to be the most glorifying to God that you can be, set your life to abide in Christ. Only as you remain close to Him are all things possible. So, in whatever you do, draw near, connect to the Vine, and give God glory, which is why the Bible says, *"Let everything that has breath praise the LORD"* (Psalm 150:6, NIV).

VISIBLE AND INVISIBLE

$\diamond$

*Who shall separate us from the love of Christ? shall
tribulation, or distress, or persecution, or famine, or
nakedness, or peril, or sword? As it is written, For thy
sake we are killed all the day long; we are accounted as
sheep for the slaughter. Nay, in all these things we are
more than conquerors through him that loved us.*

ROMANS 8:35–37, KJV

I haven't seen God, but I've seen enough of what He does
that I've got to give Him glory. When you and I give God
glory, we are reminding every demon cast out of Heaven
that they messed up. They could see Him, and they still
made the decision not to give Him glory.

God created all things, visible and invisible, all supernatural beings, all angels, all powers, all principalities, all
spiritual hosts — all of it and everything — to give Him
glory. And some of those angels, having made the decision not to do so, are now awaiting judgment. But while
they await judgment, they have taken it upon themselves
on earth to steal from God's glory.

Take a closer look at the situations and circumstances
in your life and tell me if you can't see the work of the
supernatural at play. Ephesians 6 says that we should stand

against the wiles of the devil (Ephesians 6:11). A wile is "a trick or stratagem intended to ensnare or deceive." As a verb, it is "to lure by or as if by a magic spell." [vii] It means that the enemy is constantly plotting, planning, and doing everything he can to seek your downfall.

Jesus called the devil a thief who comes to steal, kill, and destroy (John 10:10). The enemy and his legions now want to take every promise and every blessing that God has in your life. They are fallen angels who were cast out of God's presence with force. Jesus said, *"I saw Satan fall like lightning from heaven"* (Luke 10:18, NKJV).

The devil is real, but he's also limited. Have you ever heard someone say, "The devil made me do it"? That statement is simply not true. Why? Because he's not omnipotent, he's not omniscient, and he's not omnipresent. He is limited.

The devil is real, but he's also limited.

And in his limitation, he spends his time as the accuser of the brethren, bringing up your name and mine in Heavenly places, trying to tell God, "They're not worthy. They don't deserve Your love. They don't deserve Your grace. Look at them. They're behaving badly. They're talking rudely. They're doing all kinds of evil things."

Accusation, accusation, accusation. Where does he get his information? Since he's limited, he's got a team of powers and principalities and rulers over darkness. Just like God has assigned angels to you, the devil has demons out on patrol. And those demonic forces are trying to get you to stop giving God glory. The devil has commissioned them to trip people up, make them mad, keep them angry, keep them bitter — whatever it takes to torment them, harass them, and force them to turn their back on God. It's an unseen organized crime family that is working against the saints of God.

You've got to take a closer look at the problems you have in your life. Some problems are self-inflicted, yes, but some are spiritual in nature. In those cases, ask the Lord to rebuke the enemy on your behalf (Jude 1:9) and send anything that has come against you to go to uninhabited places until judgment day. Then ask the Holy Spirit to fill you once again. Don't let the gates of Hell overwhelm your heart and mind. Take a stand today for your faith, family, and future.

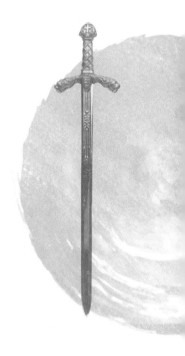

WE WRESTLE NOT

◇

If God is for us, who can be against us? He who did not spare his own Son, but gave him up for us all — how will he not also, along with him, graciously give us all things?

ROMANS 8:31–32, NIV

Next time the phone rings and the doctor says, "We need to run more tests," take a closer look and realize it may be a spiritual issue. Next time you feel treated unfairly or seeds of bitterness and rejection start to stir inside of you and poisonous emotions start to boil up in your soul, take a closer look and realize it may be manipulation by forces you cannot see.

Remember that we wrestle not against flesh and blood but against powers and principalities and hosts of wickedness in Heavenly places. You may not see them with your natural eye, but they are doing all that they can to get you to keep quiet and not give God glory for His goodness in your life.

But you need to know before anything else that Jesus has already defeated the enemy. We're not hoping for a victory; we have a victory, and that victory over the enemy has already been won by Jesus Christ.

If you read the Word, you will start to see how the unseen hand of God through the life, death, burial, and resurrection of His Son, Jesus Christ, has already accomplished all things for you.

Romans 6:11 says that though you were dead in your sin, you are now alive in Christ. Colossians 2:14 says He, *"Wiped out the handwriting of the requirements that was against us which was contrary to us. And He has taken it out of the way, having nailed it to the cross"* (NKJV). Now, when the enemy accuses you in Heaven, he's wasting air because when God hears the accusation, He turns to His Son Jesus Christ, and Jesus says, "Father, they're good with Me. My blood covers them. Take all the charges and drop them. They've been nailed to the Cross. The price has been paid."

The Bible says that Jesus has already made a public spectacle over the enemy when He defeated him at Calvary! Colossians 2:15 says, He *"disarmed principalities and powers, He made a public spectacle of them, triumphing over them in it"* (NKJV). That means Jesus won the battle more than 2,000 years ago.

The Bible says that Jesus has already made a public spectacle over the enemy when He defeated him at Calvary!

When Jesus died and said, *"It is finished,"* He went down into the bowels of the earth, and there in every crack and every chasm, in every corner of Hell, He told every demonic force, "You are defeated. You are conquered. You are crushed." Now as for you, you can say,

"Whom the Son sets free is free indeed" (John 8:36). Now if God be for us, who can be against us?

Because of Jesus, now you can also receive from God all that you need. Romans 8:32 says, *"He who did not spare His own Son, but delivered Him up for us all, how shall He not with Him also freely give us all things?"* (NKJV). Look through the lens of faith and recognize that He's still working, He's still moving, and He's still keeping His promises to you. He's still working on your family, in your physical body, and on the hope in your heart. He's alive! You can't see it, but our God is faithful! He is on His throne. He's still working, and because of Jesus, you can overcome the enemy in every area of your life (John 8:36). Now if God be for us, who can be against us?

"I am the vine, you are the branches. He who abides in Me, and I in him,

bears much fruit; for without Me you can do nothing."

JOHN 15:5 (NKJV)

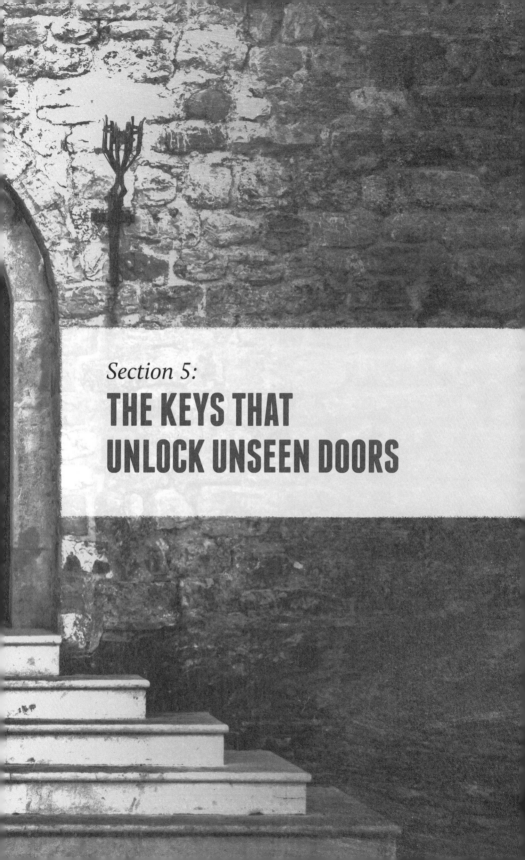

Section 5:

THE KEYS THAT UNLOCK UNSEEN DOORS

NOT ACCORDING TO FLESH

---◇---

For though we walk in the flesh, we do not war according to the flesh. For the weapons of our warfare are not carnal but mighty in God for pulling down strongholds, casting down arguments and every high thing that exalts itself against the knowledge of God, bringing every thought into captivity to the obedience of Christ.

2 CORINTHIANS 10:3-5, NKJV

Consider what the Bible has to say about the things that God has created, both visible and invisible. He has created all that there is, and He has also given you spiritual keys that will unlock every unseen door in your life. Right now, you have in your battle belt the weapons you need to push back darkness and access the things that God has in store for you.

Paul begins the conversation by reminding us that we do not walk in the flesh, and we do not war according to the flesh. You may think people are your problem, but people are not your problem. There very well could be an unseen thing that is causing people to be the problem, but we do not war according to the flesh.

What we see in the natural is not all there is to see. There are unseen realities, principalities, and powers that are active in the earth and that influence our lives. They've always been there; we just haven't had the opportunity to see them. But we do not need to fear. Paul wrote in Colossians 1:16, *"For by Him all things were created that are in heaven and that are on earth, visible and invisible, whether thrones or dominions or principalities or powers. All things were created through Him and for Him"* (NKJV). Now and forever, God reigns as King over all things.

So, when we war in the Heavenlies, we can remain mindful of who God is, what He has done, and what He has already equipped us with. We are not left unarmed, we are not left without a plan of action, and we are not left without reinforcements. And now, because of Christ's victory at the Cross, we can access everything God has already placed in store for us that the enemy is trying to keep from us.

> **We are not left unarmed, we are not left without a plan of action, and we are not left without reinforcements.**

Our battle is spiritual, and as such, we do not war according to the flesh. That means that our rules of engagement must abide by spiritual guidelines. We're engaged in unconventional warfare because our armor is spiritual, and our conflicts are supernatural. The weapons with which we engage our warfare are not carnal, meaning they are not man-made. But they are mighty in God, and they are an advanced weapons system compared to the adversary's schemes.

You have what you need. Heaven authorizes you to advance the Kingdom of God. The weapons God has issued you and me to utilize are not authorized by a denomination, a seminary course, or the authority of any man. The Creator of Heaven and earth Himself, God, the King above all kings and Lord above all lords, has authorized you and me to go weapons hot and use His Word to engage the enemy in Heavenly places. Now is the time, and today is the day, to engage in the fight and do great and mighty exploits for the Kingdom of God!

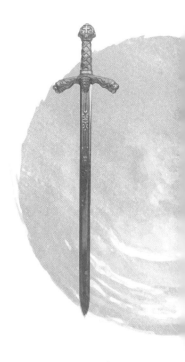

STRONGHOLDS

◇

Those who hope in the LORD will renew their strength. They will soar on wings like eagles; they will run and not grow weary, they will walk and not be faint.

ISAIAH 40:31, NIV

God has given us spiritual weapons to engage in spiritual battles to bring about results that impact both the natural and the supernatural. He has also given us authority and authorization to go and wage war on His behalf against the enemy. One of those mission objectives is to pull down strongholds. Second Corinthians 10:4 says, *"For the weapons of our warfare are not of the flesh but have divine power to destroy strongholds"* (ESV).

A stronghold, by definition, is a fortified position. It is a secure height or a retreat. [viii] Spiritually speaking, a stronghold is a place where your adversary has set up camp. And, if he's in that stronghold, he dominates that area of your life. Strongholds develop over time. People may say, "The enemy's got a stronghold on me," but I want to know why they let him stay that long?

Not only do you have the authority to pull down strongholds, but you also have the authority to *"destroy arguments and every lofty opinion raised against the knowledge of God, and take every thought captive to obey Christ"* (v. 5, ESV). The first step is to identify the battleground so you can engage the enemy. Look at what Paul says: the battle is in arguments, high things, knowledge, and thoughts.

In other words, the battleground where the enemy is going to come after you the most is in your mind. That's where he begins with his plans to steal, kill, and destroy. He wants your thought life so possessed with fear, consumed with worry, and drenched in doubt that you don't have any room left to believe anything that God has promised you.

Remember that our enemy, the serpent of old, wants to intimidate you, but he can only go so far. But 1 Peter 5:8 says, *"Be alert and of sober mind. Your enemy the devil prowls around like a roaring lion looking for someone to devour"* (NIV). He wants you to be concerned about everything that you see happening in the world, everything you hear about the government, and everything you're concerned with, so that the overwhelming strength of your life and the concerns in your heart are filled with fear, doubt, and unbelief.

> **The battleground where the enemy is going to come after you the most is in your mind.**

When those three saboteurs fill your thoughts, spiritual strongholds from the enemy's camp begin to form, build siege ramps, and strengthen in your mind. It is then easy for the enemy to keep you spiritually stagnant because you don't have the faith to believe what God has already said He would do for you. Your Bible reading goes down; your prayer life falters; and there is no praise on your lips. Consequently, you begin to live life in a downward spiral of defeat and depression.

If you feel stuck and don't know how to get out of that spiral, a helpful key is to "just start." Just start praying. Just start opening your Bible and reading. Just start lifting your voice in praise. Just start, and as you do, your inner man will begin to strengthen and your faith again will begin to spark.

In Him, you can tear down strongholds. In Him, you can rise and see your enemies scattered. In Him, you have a spirit of power, love, and a sound mind. Return once again to the Good Shepherd of your soul. In Him is all you need.

THE POWER OF DOUBT

◇

In the same way, the Spirit helps us in our weakness. We do not know what we ought to pray for, but the Spirit himself intercedes for us through wordless groans.

ROMANS 8:26, NIV

Doubt kills faith, and faith kills doubt. The enemy wants you to doubt that God's peace surpasses all understanding. Isaiah 26:3 says, *"You will keep in perfect peace those whose minds are steadfast, because they trust in you"* (NIV). God's plans for you are perfect peace and a mind at rest.

The enemy wants you to doubt that divine health belongs to the children of God. And yet, Isaiah 53:5 says, *"He was wounded for our transgressions, He was bruised for our iniquities; the chastisement for our peace was upon Him, and by His stripes we are healed"* (NKJV). Jesus already paid in full the price for your healing and peace.

The enemy wants you to doubt God's love, God's promises, and God's good plans for you. He says you're better off going your own way. But Proverbs 3:7–8 says, *"Be not wise in your own eyes; fear the LORD, and turn away from evil. It will be healing to your flesh and refreshment to your bones"* (ESV).

The enemy wants you to doubt. But if you doubt, you must realize you are going to receive nothing in return because James 1 says, *"Let him ask in faith, with no doubting, for he who doubts is like a wave of the sea driven and tossed by the wind. For let not that man suppose that he will receive anything from the Lord"* (v. 6–7, NKJV). Now I've looked up every word that means "nothing," and what it means is nothing.

And oftentimes, we read a promise in God's Word, but instead of believing it, we doubt it is really for us. If you doubt you qualify for God's blessings and promises, the enemy has a stronghold on you because Jesus has already overcome the enemy and made a way for you to come to God.

And oftentimes, we read a promise in God's Word, but instead of believing it, we doubt it is really for us.

As a father, I do not like it when my kids doubt me. And they don't know that they're doubting me, per se. But there are times when they ask questions, and the questions they ask would suggest that they're concerned about my ability to provide for them. Can you imagine what would happen if God had a bunch of sons and daughters on earth who had enough courage to take Him at His Word and believe that what He said would come to pass?

Instead of doubting and asking if God still heals people, start professing that He can cure every sickness and conquer every disease. Instead of questioning if God is still moving today, start believing that the hand of God will make a way where there seems to be no way. When you start professing what God has promised you, you will see great and mighty things that you know not!

The way we win the battle in the mind is to stop doubting God and start professing the promises of His Word. The Word of God is the most powerful weapon you own. It is the most powerful weapon on earth because it is living and active and is the very Word of God. When you appropriate the power of God's Word into your life, you are bringing a weapon to the table that cannot fail in any way. God's Word can overcome the enemy and usher you into the victory and good plans He has for you.

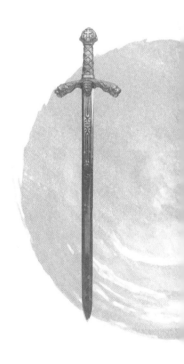

KEEPER OF THE KEYS

◇

*Jesus said to him, "If you can believe, all
things are possible to him who believes."*

MARK 9:23, NKJV

Whoever has the keys is in charge. Make no mistake about
it: Jesus Christ is Lord of all. He is the Keeper of the keys,
and He is also the Creator of the door the keys open. On the
Isle of Patmos, Jesus said, *"Do not be afraid; I am the First and
the Last. I am He who lives, and was dead, and behold, I am
alive forevermore. Amen. And I have the keys of Hades and of
Death"* (Revelation 1:17–18, NKJV).

While Jesus is King over all things, an incredible
reality is that He has also delegated authority to His
church to advance His Kingdom on the earth. At
Caesarea Philippi, Jesus said: *"I will give you the keys of
the kingdom of heaven, and whatever you bind on earth
shall be bound in heaven, and whatever you loose on
earth shall be loosed in heaven"* (Matthew 16:19, ESV).
As a believer in Christ and a grafted-in son or daugh-
ter of God, you have more authority than you realize.

So many people sit around wondering what God is
going to do about the evil agenda loose in society, the

political problems we face, or major issues around the world. They wonder what to do or hope for divine intervention, but I believe God is in Heaven, looking at His church and saying, "What are you going to do?"

We have the keys to the Kingdom. We are equipped to go and do what God has called us to do. We can humble ourselves and pray, turn from our wicked ways, and ask God to heal our land. We can bind powers and principalities on earth, so that powers and principalities will be bound in Heaven. We can release the miracle-working power of the anointing of the Living God to go forward on our behalf and defeat the enemies we face.

In Ephesians 6:18, Paul tells the church to continue *"praying always with all prayer and supplication in the Spirit, being watchful to this end with all perseverance and supplication for all the saints"* (NKJV). To be "praying always" means we need to pray more than just every now and again. God does not want us to treat Him like Uber. God wants us to completely surrender our lives to Him.

The book of James also carries another verse that says,

> **To be "praying always" means we need to pray more than just every now and again.**

"For one who knows the right thing to do and does not do it, for him it is sin" (James 4:17, NASB). So, when we connect these two verses together, we conclude that if we know we should be praying and we aren't, we see that prayerlessness is rebellion against God.

How many people are not fulfilling their mission in the Kingdom because, rather than doing what God created them to do, they're doing what they think they should do? And perhaps what they're doing isn't bad, but it's not what God put them here for. Sometimes the enemy gives you an opportunity for a "good thing" just so he can put you on the sidelines instead of seeing God use you in the unique position for which He created you. We must continually return to the Keeper of the keys, for in Him do we find His will for our lives. Let today be the day when you finally and fully put your faith in God to bring about His purposes in your life.

THE KEY OF PRAYER

——◇——

In my distress I called upon the LORD, and cried out to my God; He heard my voice from His temple, and my cry came before Him, even to His ears. Then the earth shook and trembled; the foundations of the hills also quaked and were shaken, because He was angry.

PSALM 18:6-7, NKJV

When you pray, God hears. He is not distant, and He is not far off. When David prayed and cried to the Lord in his distress, God did not leave or abandon him. No. God heard his voice and came to his rescue. God never changes and, just as He answered David's cry, so He can answer yours. And when He answers prayer, nothing can stand in His way.

Look at what happened in the New Testament church when they prayed. The Bible says, *"When they had prayed, the place in which they were gathered together was shaken, and they were all filled with the Holy Spirit and continued to speak the word of God with boldness"* (Acts 4:31, ESV). The room didn't shake until they prayed, but when they did, they felt God's power all around.

If you want God to start shaking things up in your life, start praying about the place where you want to see Him move. If you want God to shake things in your marriage, pray with your wife. If you want God to shake things with your children, lay your hands on them and pray, in faith believing, over their lives. If you want God to shake things in your business, pray at the office. Pray that God would remove every hindrance and bring every blessing. Pray that every power, principality, and weapon formed against you and any words spoken against you would fail. Because in the mighty name of Jesus, supernatural things happen when you pray.

Consider the power of prayer in the early church. In Acts 12, we read that Herod the king rose up and started harassing the church. He killed James, the brother of John, and arrested Peter during the Feast of Passover and put him in prison. Peter was bound with two chains between two soldiers assigned specifically to him, not to mention that he was *"guarded by four squads of four soldiers each"* (v. 4, NIV), on the other side of the door watching the prison, as well as the iron gate that led to the city. He had no chance of escape.

Pray that God would remove every hindrance and bring every blessing.

In light of Peter's arrest, what did the church do? They didn't panic. They didn't try to come up with a solution in their own strength and ingenuity. Instead, they gathered and interceded. The result was that the prison shook! An angel of the Lord led Peter out of the inner depths of that jail, past 16 guards, out through the gate, and down the street to freedom.

Then Peter *"came to the house of Mary, the mother of John whose surname was Mark, where many were gathered together praying"* (v. 12, NKJV). It was a miracle of a night. Whatever difficulty you're experiencing, you don't have to be confident in yourself. Rather, over any circumstance, over any situation, over any impossibility, you can be confident in God to make a way and bring you through.

CONSTANT PRAYER

◇

*Peter was therefore kept in prison, but constant
prayer was offered to God for him by the church.*

ACTS 12:5, NKJV

When the church was in dire straits and Peter was
chained in prison, three incredible words show up in
Acts 12: *"but constant prayer"* (v. 5). Where would your
life be if there wasn't constant prayer? I thank God I have
had people praying for me in difficult times and continue
to pray for me. I thank God that when the enemy tried to
come after me, I had a grandmother who was willing to
pray for me. When the enemy was using weapons against
me, I had a father who was praying for me. As I live and
breathe today, I've got a church that's praying for me. It's
constant prayer that enables us to overcome the enemy.

How many of your dreams would have been
destroyed if there wasn't constant prayer? How many
days would you have lived in sickness if there wasn't
constant prayer? How many times would you have lost
a battle if there wasn't constant prayer? What would
happen if the church today were to engage in constant
prayer until we saw mountains moved, yokes destroyed,

burdens lifted, and enemies defeated? My prayer is, "God, do it again! Do it here! And do it today, in Jesus' name!"

Peter was *"bound with two chains between two soldiers; and the guards before the door were keeping the prison"* (Acts 12:6, NKJV). But what happened? Constant prayer. Peter was asleep and under guard by four squads of four soldiers. There was no way for him to escape. But Peter had so much peace that he went to sleep. Some people can't fall asleep with three prescriptions on two mattresses, but Peter was out cold on a hard Roman floor.

That night, an angel of the Lord walked into the jail cell. Why? Because constant prayer started moving things in the Heavenly realms. The church was united in prayer, and an angel was sent to get Peter out of prison. When he showed up, he said, *"Dress yourself and put on your sandals"* (Acts 12:8, ESV).

Peter didn't question the angel. He didn't try to understand everything before he acted. He didn't try to reason before obeying. Sometimes we question God when we need to just follow orders. The angel woke Peter up, and immediately Peter got ready to go. Then he walked straight out of the prison to the house where the church was praying.

> **Sometimes we question God when we need to just follow orders.**

Peter continued knocking, *"and when they had opened the door, they saw him and were amazed"* (Acts 12:16, NASB). I want to see a church that is amazed at what God does and sees things we didn't think were possible, because that's the kind of God we serve. I want to see a church that functions in all that God has for us. When we live like that, we cannot lose because we are more than conquerors through Christ. We may be pressed, but we will not be crushed. We may be persecuted, but we will not be abandoned. We may be struck down, but we will not be destroyed. Through constant prayer, we will rise up and overcome because the weapons of our warfare are mighty in God. And when we use them in Jesus' name, we win!

THE KEY OF PRAISE

◇

Let the high praises of God be in their mouth,
and a two-edged sword in their hand.

PSALM 149:6, NKJV

One of the most potent weapons in your spiritual arsenal
is a two-edged sword. The key of praise is the comple-
ment to the key of prayer. Prayer and praise both come
out of your mouth, and both can send the enemy fleeing.
The battle is in the mind, and your words are where you
express what's in your mind.

Have you ever said to somebody, "I'm going to give
you a piece of my mind"? And what did you use? A
scalpel or your tongue? Because to give them a piece
of your mind, you had to share with them what you
were thinking. When you pray and praise, you're
telling the enemy: "You don't have a stronghold up
here. You don't have an argument up here. You don't
have anything in here that belongs to you because this
mind is submitted to the things of God." So, whenever
I encounter a difficulty, I let prayer and praise pour
out of my heart through my words.

When I see a world that's in decline, I start praising God because Philippians 4:19 says He can supply all of my needs according to His riches in glory. When I see chaos or confusion abound, I'm not worried about what anyone says because Isaiah 26:3 says He will keep them in perfect peace whose mind is stayed upon thee. I cling to Psalm 91 daily because it says that He will give His angels charge over us. And no plague will come near our dwelling.

Psalm 149:6 says, *"Let the high praises of God be in their mouth, and a two-edged sword in their hand"* (NKJV). The high praises of God do not mean that you give Him just a minor amount of appreciation. High praises mean you go after it in such a way that the world understands what you're celebrating.

Have you ever seen a fanatic? I'm talking about a baseball fanatic, a NASCAR fanatic, or a college football fanatic. They do all kinds of crazy things. You don't have to wonder about who they're supporting because it's all they talk about. But when you have the high praises of God in your mouth, you have a high view of God. He's the chief end of your thoughts, your energy, and your very life. You live your life in such a way that the world knows that you are a fanatical person when it comes to Jesus Christ.

> **High praises mean you go after it in such a way that the world understands what you're celebrating.**

When God's high praise is ever in your mouth, your life revolves around Him. You believe in Him more than you believe in anything else. You celebrate His goodness.

You celebrate His mercy. And you celebrate His faith-fulness. You're so excited about God that you can't help but shout when the world wants to be silent. The enemy may come at you one way, but you say, "This is a day for victory because the battle belongs to the Lord. The victory is mine in Christ Jesus!"

If you fill your heart and home with praise, the enemy will not be able to keep a stronghold for awfully long because if there is one thing the enemy can't stand, it's praise and worship of God Most High. Praise will bring a breakthrough. Proclaim the praises of God, and you will see that praise is what precedes victory. May the high praises of God be boldly proclaimed from your heart and mouth and may they fill your life with the wonder and power and majesty all due to God Most High.

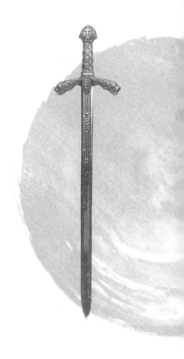

"Call to Me, and I will answer you, and show you great and mighty things,

which you do not know."

JEREMIAH 33:3 (NKJV)

WARFARE PRAYER: AN OVERVIEW

Warfare prayer is when you identify the target, and you send spiritual weapons into Heavenly places because you want to strategically strike. The target could be your marriage, your physical body, or your business. It could be your heart or your mind. Whatever it is, you can pray about it and make a difference with your prayers and your praise.

Prayer and praise are the key elements in warfare prayer. They're like a two-edged sword, sharp on both sides. But you cannot watch other people do it for you; you've got to do it yourself because as mighty and powerful as these weapons are, they are worthless if you don't use them. You have to go into your prayer closet, you have to take out your prayer list, and you have to lift your voice. When you add praise and prayer together, there is an exponential effect. Together they are like thunder and lighting, wind and rain, or the power of an atom splitting in two. When they come together, mountains move.

Right where you are, today, you can engage in warfare prayer for any situation in your life. You can raise your hands and lift your voice and start using praise as a weapon. Begin to thank God out loud for all He has done. In faith believing, ask God to pull down every stronghold, every argument, and every doubt and fear that in any way has kept you from receiving what God has already promised you through Jesus Christ, His Son, and the power of His Word.

Constant prayer, praise, and continual engagement in faith and the Word of God will push back the enemy and bring about God's purposes and plans for your life. When you engage in faith and partner with God in prayer, you will start seeing freedom and breakthrough bear witness in your life.

Every day, take a few moments and give God praise. Morning, noon, and night, open your heart to the Lord, lift your hands, and give God great and high praise. Be thankful for the things that you can see and the things you can't. Be thankful for everything that God has done in your life, great and small, because all of it is sustained by His mighty power. When you bless the name of the Lord on a daily basis, you build your inner man, draw near to God in faith believing, and you will see Heaven move on your behalf.

WARFARE PRAYER: A PRAYER

Father, in Jesus' name, we come before Your throne. Today, we declare this is the day that the Lord has made, and we will rejoice and be glad in it. We will rejoice because every answer is in You. We will rejoice because every need, You can supply.

Heavenly Father, grant abundant and full deliverance to each one right now. Let your Holy Spirit saturate our lives, and let the truth of Your Word change us, as we, through the eyes of faith, see the things that You're doing on this earth. And may we give You the glory and the honor of which You alone are worthy.

Today we will rejoice because every burden, You can lift. Every mountain, You can move. Every giant, You can defeat. We rejoice because the weapons of our warfare are not carnal but are mighty in God for pulling down strongholds. So we go into the Heavenly places, and we announce to powers and principalities, in the name of Jesus that they are defeated, and Christ has won every victory. And by the blood of the Lamb, the works of the enemy have been, are being, and will be destroyed.

I pray for every person reading right now, for their families, and for everyone they are interceding for. I pray for all who are sick in their body and for all who need Your hand to intervene — that the power of the mighty name of Jesus can and will heal today. Every person struggling in their marriage, I declare that what God has brought together, let no man put asunder, but may healing and reconciliation pour out like waves on the shore and bring with them the refreshing of Heaven.

I pray in the mighty name of Jesus that every demonic force of Hell that has attacked every home will be destroyed. I pray for every businessman and every businesswoman, and every child of God who's looking for sufficiency —I declare that El Shaddai is an all-sufficient God who owns the cattle on a thousand hills, and He will bring about all supply. And He is moving it into the hands of His children who will put their trust in Him. May He do great and mighty things in your life, in your family, and in the dreams of your heart. Today, Lord, bring about a great victory and breakthrough over every area of our lives.

May the enemy that's attacking your life be defeated. May the enemy that's attacking your storehouse be destroyed. And may the enemy that's trying to keep you in doubt, unbelief, or fear be cut off in the mighty name of Jesus. May they be cast to uninhabited places until judgment day.

But as for you as a child of God, you have a promise in His Word: *"No good thing does he withhold from those who walk uprightly"* (Psalm 84:11, NKJV). Now Father, bless us and keep us. Make Your face to shine upon us and be gracious unto us. Let the lens of Your truth always bring us vision and insight to what Your hand is doing in the world around us.

And let us ever be mindful of the day in which we live, knowing that though we engage in the battle, the victory has come through Christ our Savior. And may we be ever confident that You are fighting for us, standing beside us, and working in us, and that nothing is impossible to those who believe. And may You exceedingly and abundantly bless each one praying today and may You bring to completion the good work You have begun in their lives.

IN JESUS' NAME, AMEN.

ENDNOTES

i.   https://hymnary.org/text/o_soul_are_you_weary_and_troubled

ii.   https://www.merriam-webster.com/dictionary/violence

iii.   https://www.merriam-webster.com/dictionary/commission

iv.   https://biblehub.com/greek/225.htm

v.   https://webbtelescope.org

vi.   https://www.washington.edu/news/2022/12/08/southern-ring-nebula

vii.   https://www.merriam-webster.com/dictionary/wiles

viii.   https://biblehub.com/hebrew/4869.htm

ABOUT THE AUTHOR

Pastor Matt Hagee is the Lead Pastor of the 22,000 member Cornerstone Church in San Antonio, Texas, where he partners with his father, founder Pastor John Hagee. Pastor Matt and his wife Kendal are committed to sharing the Gospel of Jesus Christ with the nations of the world and committed to building bridges between generations.

Since graduating from Oral Roberts University, Pastor Matt has authored eight books, founded an award-winning Gospel music group and completed his graduate studies at Texas A&M University College Station.

He and his wife Kendal share weekly messages of encouragement through their television program, *The Difference* and the *Matt and Kendal Hagee* podcast. They are blessed with four beautiful children and enjoy every opportunity that they have to spend time together at their home in Boerne, Texas.

TO LEARN MORE ABOUT
PASTOR MATT HAGEE AND HAGEE MINISTRIES, VISIT:

HAGEE MINISTRIES:
jhm.org

FACEBOOK:
HageeMinistries
mattandkendalhagee

TWITTER:
PastorMattHagee
HageeMinistries

INSTAGRAM:
MattHagee
HageeMinistries